W9-BSV-171

THE LITTLE BOOK OF
Strategic
Peacebuilding

Published titles include:

The Little Book of Restorative Justice: Revised & Updated,
by Howard Zehr
The Little Book of Conflict Transformation,
by John Paul Lederach
The Little Book of Family Group Conferences,
New-Zealand Style, by Allan MacRae and Howard Zehr
The Little Book of Strategic Peacebuilding, by Lisa Schirch
The Little Book of Strategic Negotiation,
by Jayne Seminare Docherty
The Little Book of Circle Processes, by Kay Pranis
The Little Book of Contemplative Photography, by Howard Zehr
The Little Book of Restorative Discipline for Schools,
by Lorraine Stutzman Amstutz and Judy H. Mullet
The Little Book of Trauma Healing, by Carolyn Yoder
The Little Book of Biblical Justice, by Chris Marshall
The Little Book of Restorative Justice for People in Prison,
by Barb Toews
The Little Book of Cool Tools for Hot Topics,
by Ron Kraybill and Evelyn Wright
El Pequeño Libro De Justicia Restaurativa, by Howard Zehr
The Little Book of Dialogue, by Lisa Schirch and David Campt
The Little Book of Victim Offender Conferencing,
by Lorraine Stutzman Amstutz
The Little Book of Restorative Justice for Sexual Abusers and Their
Victims, by Judah Oudshoorn with Michelle Jackett and Lorraine
Stutzman Amstutz
The Big Book of Restorative Justice: Three Classic Justice & Peace-
building Books in One Volume, by Howard Zehr,
Lorraine S. Amstutz, Allan Macrae, and Kay Pranis

The Little Books of Justice & Peacebuilding
present, in highly accessible form, key concepts and
practices from the fields of restorative justice, conflict transformation, and peacebuilding. Written by leaders in these
fields, they are designed for practitioners, students, and anyone interested in justice, peace, and conflict resolution.
The Little Books of Justice & Peacebuilding
series is a cooperative effort between the Center for Justice
and Peacebuilding of Eastern Mennonite University and publisher Good Books.

THE LITTLE BOOK OF
Strategic Peacebuilding

A Vision and Framework for Peace with Justice

LISA SCHIRCH

Good Books

New York, New York

Cover photograph by Howard Zehr

Design by Dawn J. Ranck

THE LITTLE BOOK OF STRATEGIC PEACEBUILDING
Copyright © 2004 by Good Books, an imprint of Skyhorse Publishing, Inc.
International Standard Book Number: 978-1-56148-427-0
Library of Congress Catalog Card Number: 2004018364

All rights reserved. No part of this book may be reproduced in any manner
without the express written consent of the publisher, except in the case of
brief excerpts in critical reviews or articles. All inquiries should be addressed
to Good Books, 307 West 36th Street, 11th Floor, New York, NY 10018.

Good Books books may be purchased in bulk at special discounts for sales
promotion, corporate gifts, fund-raising, or educational purposes. Special
editions can also be created to specifications. For details, contact the Special
Sales Department, Good Books, 307 West 36th Street, 11th Floor, New York,
NY 10018 or info@skyhorsepublishing.com.

Good Books in an imprint of Skyhorse Publishing, Inc.®,
a Delaware corporation.

Visit our website at www.goodbooks.com.

10 9 8 7 6 5

Library of Congress Cataloging-in-Publication Data

Schirch, Lisa.
  The little book of strategic peacebuilding / by Lisa Schirch.
    p. cm.
  Includes bibliographical references.
  ISBN 1-56148-427-X (pbk.)
  1. Peace-building. 2. Conflict management. I. Title.
  JZ5538.S35 2004
  303.6'9--dc22   2004018364

Printed in the United States of America

Table of Contents

Acknowledgments

Most of the content in this book grew out of reflecting and learning with thousands of students and practitioners who have touched our lives at the Conflict Transformation Program at Eastern Mennonite University (EMU) in Harrisonburg, VA. I deeply appreciate the efforts of many students and friends who read and responded to drafts of this book, especially Rob Davis, Larrisa Fast, Debendra Manandhar, Toma Ragnjiya, Katie Resendiz, Maria Schirch de Sanchez, and Yashodha Shrestha. I also thank two of my colleagues, Howard Zehr and John Paul Lederach, for investing time toward mentoring me in this field and for helping me make important decisions about the content of this book.

I began working on this text while living in Nairobi, Kenya, in March 2003, just as the U.S.-led war on Iraq was beginning. I want to thank my husband and daughter for reminding me during the day to turn off the BBC news of the war, to walk away from my laptop where I was writing about peace, and to take a walk with them among the giraffes and zebras near our apartment to experience the beauty of this precious life that we live and work to preserve. Although peacebuilding aims to save the world, we must also remember to *savor* it.

1.
Introduction

A group of people affected by violence in their community meet together to talk with each other and plan their response. A police officer works with community members to patrol the streets at night to prevent crime. A women's group blockades the exit in the negotiation room where rebel groups are trying to withdraw from peace talks. A researcher interviews government ministers about the effect of civil society actors like churches, development organizations, and women's groups on recent democratic elections. These are among the thousands of people who engage in building peace. They work not just to end violence but to create structures that contribute to a just and sustainable peace.

The field of peacebuilding is wider and more complex than most people realize. It encompasses actors in many different arenas: community members searching for a better life; nonviolent activists pushing for human rights; peacekeepers separating groups in conflict and demobilizing combatants; religious leaders encouraging their followers to make peace with neighbors; relief workers bringing aid; community mediators and restorative justice practitioners who facilitate dialogue between conflicting parties; business leaders giving material aid to victims; and government leaders initiating change through public policy. These are just a few actors in peacebuilding.

These actors use different languages to talk about their values and describe their activities. They have different theories of how social change happens, and they have different roles and responsibilities in society. For example, some speak of the need for law and order, others of spiritual healing, human rights and social justice, a return to traditional values, conflict resolution skills, development, education, or a combination of all of the above. In practice, they may work in the same region, yet they may never coordinate their approaches. Building a just and sustainable peace requires that the various actors and actions are coordinated into an overarching framework.

Why this *Little Book*?

This *Little Book* is an attempt to bring together the various fields and activities related to peacebuilding to integrate them into one conceptual framework. At the core of this framework is the idea of *strategic peacebuilding,* an interdisciplinary, coordinated approach to building a sustainable *justpeace*—a peace with justice.

Strategic peacebuilding requires clear goals. While the concept of justpeace is growing in popularity, few writings lay out the vision and practice of it. One aim of this book is to promote the concept of justpeace as an overall goal or vision for peacebuilding.

Strategic peacebuilding also requires coordination. While some peacebuilding scholars focus on how to directly affect the people in conflict, this book adds a focus on how people working for peace need to network with each other. It attempts to synthesize and summarize the values, relational skills, analytical frameworks, and practices of a wide range of peacebuilding actors. This synthesis aims to create a common language for talking about peacebuilding and to increase awareness and appreciation of the important and diverse roles involved.

The framework presented here has emerged out of the thoughts and experiences of thousands of people and networks from around the world who are connected to the Conflict Transformation Program at Eastern Mennonite University. It gathers wisdom from progressives and conservatives, from Northerners and Southerners in the global community, from actions of the past and voices of the future in an attempt to fit these diverse paths into a coherent peacebuilding map.

I hope that this book can serve as a primer for students and others who are interested in learning about the field of peacebuilding. It is also written for practitioners and academics who may know about one part of the peacebuilding puzzle but would benefit from learning more about other approaches and how these fit together.

In short, this *Little Book* attempts to provide a more unified and strategic vision of peacebuilding. It seeks to show how the various approaches to peacebuilding connect and together contribute to addressing violence while bringing about long-term structural change.

2.
Defining Strategic Peacebuilding

The field of peacebuilding, like any field, has an audience of cheerleaders, critics, and confused onlookers. People use the term "peacebuilding" in widely differing ways. Some use it to describe activities following a war. Others use it to define a new way of approaching development with an emphasis on peace. Still others see peacebuilding as mainly a relational and psychological process or use it interchangeably with the idea of conflict transformation. This chapter explores the myths and meanings of peacebuilding.

The field of peacebuilding developed in response to the world's most severe cases of violence: widespread and growing poverty; increased crime, racism, and oppression; violence against women; and wars like the ones in Liberia or Colombia, where ethnic, ideological, and class divisions are fueled by a thriving global arms trade. Any answer to the question "What is being done about these problems?" is potentially part of peacebuilding.

Peacebuilding seeks to prevent, reduce, transform, and help people recover from violence in all forms, even structural violence that has not yet led to massive civil unrest. At the same time, it empowers people to foster relationships at all levels that sustain them and their environment.

Peacebuilding supports the development of relationships at all levels of society: between individuals and within families; communities; organizations; businesses; governments; and cultural, religious, economic, and political institutions and movements. Relationships are a form of power or *social capital*. When people connect and form relationships, they are more likely to cooperate together to constructively address conflict.

Peace does not just happen. It is built when people take great care in their decision-making to plan for the long term, anticipating potential problems, engaging in ongoing analysis of the conflict and local context, and coordinating different actors and activities in all stages of conflict and at all levels of society. Strategic peacebuilding recognizes the complexity of the tasks required to build peace. Peacebuilding is strategic when resources, actors, and approaches are coordinated to accomplish multiple goals and address multiple issues for the long term.

Peacebuilding is *not* . . .

- **Peacebuilding is not soft or idealistic.**

For many people, the idea of peace is a farfetched dream in a world full of violence. While strategic peacebuilding works toward a long-term vision of a just peace, it is also based on a realistic appraisal of the complex challenges in the immediate context. Peacebuilders face the challenge to be politically strategic in the present while at the same time basing their work in a set of values and principles that meet long-term goals.

- **Peacebuilding is not the same as conflict transformation.**
  Conflict mitigation, management, resolution, and transformation use similar sets of skills and processes designed to build relationships and address the roots of conflict through dialogue, mediation, and negotiation. But the field of peacebuilding includes a far wider variety of processes.

- **Peacebuilding is not only for post-war societies.**
  Peacebuilding needs to take place in all societies as a way to prevent violence and satisfy human needs. Preventive peacebuilding, also known as *conflict prevention,* aims to create societies that can address conflict without violence.

- **Peacebuilding is not based primarily on Western ideas.**
  The values, skills, analytical tools, and processes of peacebuilding are truly global. Every culture has something to teach as well as learn about peacebuilding. Many peacebuilding processes such as restorative justice, mediation, and nonviolent action were adapted to the West from elsewhere.

- **Peacebuilding does not avoid conflict or ignore structural forms of violence and injustice.**
  Some criticize the field of peacebuilding for "ambulance driving," or responding to crises rather than work-

ing to prevent violence. In the strategic peacebuilding framework presented in this book, the important roles of preventing violence and creating just social structures go hand-in-hand.

Strategic Peacebuilding is a Connecting Space

The diagram on page 12 illustrates some of the many approaches to peacebuilding. Peacebuilding requires a combination of approaches to peace through a connecting space or nexus for collaboration.

This diagram illustrates approaches to peace rather than actors or issues. Some actors may use several approaches, such as education, economic development, and conflict transformation processes to address many different issues related to conflict, such as HIV/AIDS or environmental pollution. This diagram gives a sampling of some of the approaches addressed in this book.

Each approach makes a unique contribution and complements other approaches. Part of the challenge of peacebuilding is holding together the vision for how these different approaches contribute to peace. Peacebuilding actors may not know about how other approaches could contribute to their own work, or how they can contribute to the work of others.

The concept of "creating space" for peacebuilding is a key strategic principle. Often, there is no physical space where people working toward peace can coordinate their work and share their successes and challenges. The visual diagram of a nexus creates a meeting place or space for this important coordination and exchange between approaches.

The intersection of approaches reflects a set of *values, relational skills, analytical frameworks,* and *processes.*

The next chapters discuss these values, skills, analytical frameworks, and processes in more detail.

Nexus of Peacebuilding Approaches

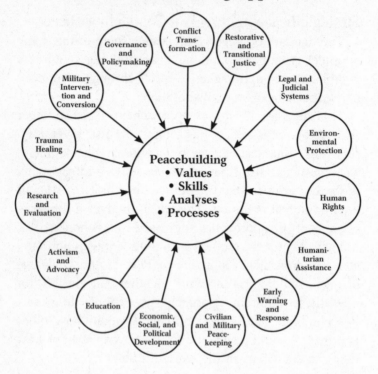

3.
Values for Peacebuilding

Peacebuilding grows out of a set of values. Values guide all decision-making. Ideally, people begin building peace by reflecting on how their lives and choices impact others. When people work with others to build peace, their values are often hidden or unstated. But values can be revealed by a key question about goals: What will peacebuilding accomplish? In general, peacebuilding values meeting human needs and protecting human rights.

Human Needs and Human Rights

Peacebuilding values the quality and sustainability of life. Peacebuilding aims to create societies that affirm human dignity through meeting human needs and protecting human rights. Peacebuilders also have a responsibility to protect the environment.

From the time of the earliest civilizations until today, most religious traditions have promoted relationships that meet human needs. The introduction of human rights charters after World War II increased the expectation that governments should address human needs by protecting and promoting human rights laws.

Humans have material, social, and cultural needs and rights.[1] Human rights serve as a moral guide for people at every level of society. They give direction for making all types of decisions about how people can live with the least amount of violence and the greatest amount of common good.

- **Material needs and rights** include food, shelter, water, healthcare, and resources to meet physical needs. They require societies to protect economic rights through distributive justice or a fair distribution of wealth, education, and employment opportunities for all people.

- **Social needs and rights** include a sense of human dignity, belonging and predictability in relationships, security from attack, participation and influence in making decisions that affect one's life, and an ability to earn respect and recognition from others. They require societies to protect social, civil, and political rights through procedural justice. This includes democratic structures, the enforcement of the rule of law, and social justice programs of empowerment and education that foster cross-cultural understanding.

- **Cultural needs and rights** include the ability to give life meaning through personal, cultural, and religious identities without persecution, threats, or intimidation. Cultures and religions give people a sense of meaning, purpose, and identity. These needs and rights require societies to protect religious freedoms, minority rights, and other social and civil rights through laws and education programs that foster understanding and tolerance.

People have choices about how to satisfy their needs. Everyone needs food, but not everyone needs to eat the same foods. Everyone needs respect, but people earn and give respect in different ways. Humans often want to satisfy their needs in the same ways other people do. They imitate the desires of others, particularly of those deemed to be powerful, in an effort to belong to their group.[2]

Sometimes it is hard to distinguish need from greed. Some people perceive that they have the right to meet their own needs at the expense of others. Greed is the desire to accumulate excessive amounts of material resources, decision-making power, and respect. An internalized sense of superiority and greed create an excessive sense of need.

Peacebuilding requires an ethic of *interdependence, partnership,* and *limiting violence* when making choices about how to satisfy needs and protect rights.

Interdependence

Humans are interdependent; the unmet human needs or rights of any individual or group ripple outward and affect the whole of humanity. When people are aware of and value interdependence with others, they coordinate efforts to meet human needs and rights so that they do not harm others. The world's wealthy people, for example, cannot meet all of their needs, particularly for security, in a world where others' basic human needs go unmet.

Partnership

A dominate-or-be-dominated worldview creates a foundation for violence. The value of partnership is an alternative to domination. It encourages people to use power *with* others to satisfy mutual needs and rights. When relationships are egalitarian and based on the values of partnership rather than domination, people cooperate with and empower each other to meet their needs and rights.

Limiting Violence

Humans hurt each other in many ways through choices they make about what or what not to consume, how to interact with others, and when to use force against others to meet needs. Conflicts will occur as people pursue both liberty and security, both private property and distributive justice. Any use of violence to pursue the human needs and rights of one person or group harms and obstructs the rights of others. A cycle of violence results when individuals and groups use violence against each other.

Levels of violence or harm fall along a continuum. Peacebuilding is about increasing the number of nonviolent options people believe they have to satisfy their needs and helping them choose the least violent options.

The concepts of *justice, justpeace,* and *human security* express peacebuilding values. *Justice* exists when people are able to participate in shaping their environment so that they can meet their needs. Justice exists when people respect the human rights of others, and when there are processes in place for holding people who violate the rights of others accountable to their victims and to the wider community.

The concept of *justpeace* recognizes that justice pursued violently only contributes to further injustice, and that peace without justice is unlikely to be sustainable.

Human security exists when people are safe from direct and structural forms of violence and are able to meet their basic needs and rights. Human security advocates seek to replace or broaden traditional state-based definitions of security that focus on protecting territory or national interests. Human security aims to reduce the threats of disease, poverty, crime, and other factors that lessen the quality of life.

While the language here is secular to reflect the broad readership of this book, religious groups have their own ways of communicating these concepts. People of many faiths understand the pursuit of peace, justice, and reconciliation between people as God's will for humanity. Peacebuilding is also a religious task and includes an important spiritual dimension.

The values described here guide peacebuilding. Individuals and organizations can make decisions and assess their work with the help of these values. Chapter 11 describes how these values can help shape the practice of peacebuilding. Yet values alone are not enough. Relational skills help people behave in ways that reflect these values.

4.
Relational Skills
for Peacebuilding

Conflict is a natural part of all relationships. Peacebuilding addresses the big conflicts between armed groups as well as the little, everyday conflicts that occur in the course of living and working in organizations and communities. Conflict happens as communities decide where to dig a well, which school curriculum to use, and which leader to elect. Conflict happens among peacebuilders as they seek funding for their projects, as they negotiate with each other about opportunities, and as they seek recognition for their work.

Groups in conflict often experience high levels of internal conflict that, in turn, hamper efforts to address opposing groups. All too often, high-level leaders come to the negotiation table without a mandate from the people they represent. People working in the field of peacebuilding who are not able to learn and practice these skills in all of their relationships are severely hampered in their ability to build peace.

The following relational skills allow people to address conflict in constructive ways:

- **Self-reflection skills** help people to gain insight into their own behavior patterns in relationships with others and to identify healthy life choices. These skills allow people to adapt to varying circumstances and contexts and to experience a sense of peace within themselves.

- **Active listening skills** help people to use verbal and nonverbal ways to check for understanding and to show attention and respect for other people's experiences and perceptions.

- **Diplomatic and assertive speaking skills** help people to communicate about important or potentially conflictual issues in tactful ways that are easier for others to hear and understand.

- **Appreciative inquiry skills** help people to identify their strengths and successes as a way to build on what works well in their relationships with others.

- **Creative problem-solving skills** help people to brainstorm and to discover new ways to solve difficult problems.

- **Dialogue skills** help diverse individuals and groups to communicate honestly to achieve mutual understanding and transformation.

- **Negotiation skills** help people to learn to assert their own needs while understanding that a sustainable solution also requires addressing the needs of others.

- **Mediation skills** help people to guide others through the process of negotiation to develop mutually satisfactory solutions.

These skills primarily come out of the fields of conflict transformation, restorative justice, and trauma healing, discussed in Chapter 9. Relational skills are the foundation of all democratic processes, where individuals can participate in making important decisions that affect their lives. They are like grease to the wheels of peacebuilding. Without them, peacebuilding crumbles to interpersonal squabbles among peacebuilders, angry crowds shouting messages of hate, and political decisions made purely on the basis of power rather than on human needs. Yet relational skills are not enough. Analytical frameworks, explored in the next chapter, add yet another dimension to our understanding of peacebuilding.

5.
Analysis for Peacebuilding

Conflict and violence are always complex. Analytical tools help organize what we know about conflict in a way that lets us identify where to intervene in it. The many analytical tools useful for peacebuilding go beyond the scope of this book. However, it is important to note three key analytical principles for addressing the roots of conflict.

Understand the local context.

Peacebuilders need to know what the conflict is about, who is affected or involved in the conflict, what needs to stop, what divides and connects people, and what fosters vulnerability to conflict. The more peacebuilders know about a context, the more likely they will be successful in contributing to peace.

People who use violence always find a way to justify it.

People who cannot satisfy their material, social, or cultural needs often feel a sense of *injustice* and/or *trau-*

ma. When people perceive that others humiliate them or commit an injustice against them, they often are willing to fight and even die to protect their physical, social, or cultural identity.

Conflict occurs when people perceive that some want to satisfy their needs in a way that obstructs or threatens the needs of others. Conflict can be handled constructively or destructively. Conflict is constructive when people develop ways to satisfy the needs of all involved. People may resort to violence if they feel little empathy for others and are not able to identify nonviolent ways of meeting their needs. *Violence* occurs when people address conflict in a way that harms or destroys relationships by frustrating or denying the human needs of others.

Violence is an attempt to do justice or undo injustice. A child soldier in Uganda may join rebels as a way to find belonging and identity—or even food. A rebel leader may use violence to obtain higher status and more wealth. Peacebuilding requires identifying the perceptions of unmet needs in order to find alternative, nonviolent ways to satisfy those needs.

All forms of violence are related.

Structural violence refers to the disabilities, disparities, and even deaths that result when systems, institutions, or policies meet some people's needs and rights at the expense of others. Structures that foster disparity and satisfy the needs of people from one ethnic, religious, class, age, language, or gender group at the expense of others propagate violence. The growing number of failed or dysfunctional governments signals the inability of some states to provide an environment where people can meet their basic needs. Societies that permit or encourage economic and social disparity, exclude some groups from full participation in decision-making and public life, or direct harm toward some people suffer more from all forms of violence. When structures are violent, they infect entire cultures.

Structural violence often leads to *secondary violence,* which includes civil wars, crime, domestic violence, substance abuse, and suicide. These result in part when structural violence creates vast disparities in the satisfaction of human needs and rights. Many criminal acts that personally humiliate and victimize others grow out of structural violence. A clear correlation exists between people in prison and people who grew up in poverty and/ or abusive homes and experienced few opportunities, constant humiliation, and little chance to gain respect. Disparities in income and wealth between the rich and the poor are the most powerful predictors of homicide rates in any city, state, or country.[3]

People who are unable to find constructive ways to meet their own needs end up creating an endless cycle of victimization. Different forms of violence spread like a virus. The diagram on page 24 shows the connection between structural violence and the three main forms of secondary violence that result from it.

These three analytical principles provide a background for exploring the range of peacebuilding processes. Successful peacebuilding processes can harness both local and external resources to prevent and reduce violence, and to transform and help people recover from it. Chapter 11 on the "Strategic Design of Peacebuilding" provides more analytical tools for deciding on which particular process is useful in each unique context. The next chapters explore the wide range of processes that help build peace.

Structural Violence

Disparities, disabilities, and deaths result when systems, institutions, policies, or cultural beliefs meet some people's human needs and human rights at the expense of others. Structural violence creates relationships that cause secondary violence to occur.

Secondary Violence

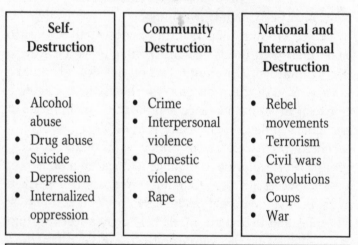

Self-Destruction	Community Destruction	National and International Destruction
• Alcohol abuse • Drug abuse • Suicide • Depression • Internalized oppression	• Crime • Interpersonal violence • Domestic violence • Rape	• Rebel movements • Terrorism • Civil wars • Revolutions • Coups • War

Reactions and responses to structural violence are secondary violence.

6.
An Overview of Peacebuilding Processes

Peacebuilding requires a range of approaches. The approaches included in the peacebuilding nexus can be grouped into four categories that focus on specific tasks.

Waging Conflict Nonviolently

Advocates and activists seek to gain support for change by increasing a group's power to address issues and ripen the conditions needed to transform relationships.

Reducing Direct Violence

Efforts to reduce direct violence aim to restrain perpetrators of violence, prevent and relieve the immediate suffering of victims of violence, and create a safe space for peacebuilding activities. Once this happens other processes can address the root causes of the violence.

Transforming Relationships

For peace to replace violence, relationships must be re-created by using an array of processes that address trauma, transform conflict, and do justice. These processes give people opportunities to create long-term, sustainable solutions to address their needs.

Building Capacity

Longer-term peacebuilding efforts capitalize on existing capacities to meet needs and rights. Efforts include preventing violence through education and training, development, military conversion and transformation, and research and evaluation. These activities aim to build just structures that support a sustainable culture of peace.

Map of Peacebuilding

Waging Conflict Nonviolently

- Monitoring and advocacy
- Direct action
- Civilian-based defense

Building Capacity

- Training and education
- Development
- Military conversion
- Research and evaluation

Reducing Direct Violence

- Legal and justice systems
- Humanitarian assistance
- Peacekeeping
- Military intervention
- Cease-fire agreements
- Peace zones
- Early warning programs

Transforming Relationships

- Trauma healing
- Conflict transformation
- Restorative justice
- Transitional justice
- Governance and policymaking

While many actors engage in multiple categories of peacebuilding, this map highlights the unique goals of different peacebuilding approaches. These approaches are often simultaneous, ongoing, and interdependent. The next four chapters explore the purpose and functions of each of these circles to show how they provide complementary contributions to peacebuilding.

7.
Waging Conflict Nonviolently

In conflicts where power is unbalanced and there is little public awareness of the issues, it is often difficult to get conflicting parties to negotiate. Those who agree to dialogue under these conditions often find it unsatisfying, as groups with more power may not negotiate in good faith or make the necessary structural changes. In such cases, it may be important to wage conflict nonviolently through strategic nonviolence.

Nonviolent action aims to raise awareness and balance power.

Strategic nonviolence is a set of approaches that works for change by escalating the conflict without using violence. Far from being passive, strategic nonviolence is a direct and assertive form of addressing conflict. Nonviolent action aims to raise public awareness and sympathy, increase understanding of how groups in conflict are interdependent, and balance power by convincing or coercing others to accept the needs or desires of all involved.

People decide to use nonviolent action instead of violence for different reasons. Strategic arguments point to the ineffectiveness of violent actions throughout history.[4] Others see nonviolent action as effective because it is relatively less expensive than using violence. In Latin America, nonviolence is called the weapon of the poor. Planning a demonstration, vigil, strike, or boycott does not require expensive weapons. Still others, particularly those from religious bases, assert that nonviolence is a morally superior method of struggle. Mahatma Gandhi and Martin Luther King Jr. argued that peace cannot be achieved through violence; there must be harmony between the means used to attain an end.

Whatever the rationale, the strategy of nonviolence depends upon satisfying the needs of all people: defenders and offenders. This mutual satisfaction of needs can happen by creating nonviolent expressions of power to pressure for successful negotiation, and by limiting the power of others to obstruct needs and rights.

Creating Power

Militaries increase their power through the quantity and quality of their weapons and troops. Groups using nonviolence increase their power through tactics that demonstrate how others depend upon their cooperation.

A government's political power, for example, ultimately depends upon the consent and cooperation of its citizens and, at times, the world community. The world community applied economic and cultural sanctions on South Africa in the 1980s. These demonstrated South Africa's dependence on the world community and pressured the white government to change. Within South Africa, black communities boycotted white stores in a similar show of white dependency on blacks. These strategies contributed to the end of apartheid in South Africa.

The *Aikido* Principle

The principles of Aikido, a nonviolent martial art, help to conceptualize how the opposition's power can be used to defeat it. In *Aikido* fighting, a defender pulls or pushes the attacker in the same direction he/she is moving, rather than resisting or blocking the attack. This throws the attacker off balance as he/she expects resistance. An attacker's own force leads to failure to dominate and control the *Aikido* practitioner.

Nonviolent action exposes the opponent's violence both to themselves and to the world community. When white policemen beat and used dogs against protesters, including children, during the Civil Rights movement, people in the United States and around the world immediately responded with outrage. The white policemen showed themselves and the world what a system of racial segregation required. Their own violent actions led to their downfall.

Gene Sharp lists almost 200 different nonviolent tactics to wage conflict nonviolently.[5] These tactics belong to one of four categories: monitoring and advocacy, protest and persuasion, non-cooperation, and intervention.

Nonviolent Tactics for Waging Conflict
Monitoring and Advocacy

Some groups escalate conflict nonviolently by monitoring issues and advocating for change. Human rights and environmental groups, for example, monitor the way states, corporations, and other groups protect human rights and the environment. These reports both raise public awareness of abuses and create a record of rights abuses that may serve other peacebuilding processes, such as negotiations that require objective criteria for determining harms.

Amnesty International uses the phrase "the mobilization of shame" to capture the dynamic that occurs when organizations mobilize large numbers of people to denounce or shame a state, business, or group into changing its behavior. Mobilizing shame is a way to raise public awareness and increase an organization's power to bring about change.[6]

Shaming *behaviors* rather than *people* is important, as the goal of shaming is to change behavior and not simply to isolate groups that already reject a sense of interdependence with others. Isolation can backfire if as groups become even more entrenched in an ideology of us vs. them and escalate their use of violence against others.

Protest and Persuasion

This approach aims to raise awareness of injustice and bring shame to perpetrators of violence through public acts such as publications, speeches, marches, or symbolic mock funerals to call attention to people who have died. In Kenya's 2002 elections, for example, civil society organizations plastered walls with posters and announced on radio programs that everyone was responsible for creating peaceful elections. This contributed to a historic change in leadership and reduced the number of election-related deaths.

Non-Cooperation

This type of nonviolent action centers on acts of omission, where people stop doing their normal activities as a way to resist another group. Sharp identifies three types of non-cooperation.[7] *Social non-cooperation* includes boycotts of sporting or social events, school strikes by students, or emigration from a city or state. *Economic non-cooperation* includes consumer boycotts, refusal to pay rent, withdrawal of bank deposits or investments, worker strikes or work slow-downs, and applying sanctions or embargoes on offending governments and businesses. *Political non-cooperation* includes boycotts of elections or government offices; civil disobedience of unjust laws, such as apartheid; and refusal to recognize government authority.

Civilian defense employs a strategy of non-cooperation to defend against military aggression. It uses unarmed civilians in conjunction with or instead of a military to defend against attack. Civilian defense works by refusing to cooperate with invaders.

During World War II, Denmark was the only country to successfully save a majority of their Jewish population while actively resisting Nazi occupation. When Nazis forced Jewish Danes to wear the yellow star, non-Jewish Danes wore the star in solidarity with Jews. The night before the Nazis were to begin taking Jewish people to the death camps, Danish civilians coordinated a massive strategy to hide Jewish people and move them out of the country on fishing boats.

The Danes also used work strikes, symbolic moments of silence, sabotage of their own railway systems, and other nonviolent means to make Nazi occupation of their country difficult and unrewarding. Meanwhile, the Danes protected their local culture and resisted their occupiers through singing Danish folk songs and staging supportive demonstrations of the Danish King and government while Nazi soldiers marched in their streets.[8] This example from Denmark shows how civilian defense prevents invaders from benefiting from their occupation.

Intervention

This strategy aims to interrupt the status quo and draw attention to violence as a way to mobilize people for change. *Psychological intervention* uses fasts, exposure to the elements, or danger to pressure people's moral systems. *Physical intervention* involves sitting, standing, lying down, singing, or doing some action as a way to invade and occupy public space. *Social intervention* includes group meetings, Internet networking, phone trees, public drama and theater, or strategic interruptions of normal life, such as overloading public facilities like buses or phone lines. *Economic intervention* includes nonviolent seizure of assets and of land and creating alternative economic trading systems or markets. *Political intervention* includes seeking imprisonment, overloading government facilities, and setting up parallel governments.

Nonviolent action alone cannot build peace. It escalates conflict and can often temporarily increase antagonism and tension between people and groups. Governments and other groups in power may escalate the use of violent repression on groups waging conflict nonviolently in an effort to stop them. However, activities to wage conflict nonviolently ideally ripen the conditions for transforming relationships and structures. In many cases, this is essential as structures resist change, and people in power may ignore pleas for dialogue or negotiation. The next chapters look at other pieces of the peacebuilding puzzle that, together, form a united vision for moving toward a justpeace.

8.
Reducing
Direct Violence

The second category of strategic peacebuilding process-es includes state-based legal and judicial systems, the military, and civilian peacekeeping efforts and programs such as refugee camps and shel-ters to give people a safe place to live. These programs interrupt the cycle of violence and lay the foun-dation for further peacebuilding in three ways: preventing victim-ization, restraining offenders, and creating safe space.

> These strategies aim to prevent victimization, restrain offenders, and make a safe space for other peacebuilding pro-cesses.

Preventing Victimization

In many civil wars, civilians are targeted as a strategy of war. Civilian massacres plant the seeds for future wars and revenge killings. In Rwanda and Burundi, the international community failed to act when warned of impending genocide. Once the killings started, the cycle of violence became a raging flood that affected every street in every village. If international peacekeepers had been there to prevent the victimization of civilians, far fewer people would have died, and far fewer people would have taken up arms to conduct revenge killings on civilians of the opposing ethnic group. The more peacebuilders can protect civilians from becoming victims, the more likely they are to prevent an expansion of war and direct violence.

Restraining Offenders

People who commit crimes or attack civilians need to be stopped. The Western legal framework uses state-based law enforcement and justice processes to protect citizens from individuals who are not able or willing to follow laws. While this approach is not always successful—and indeed can be counterproductive—a system of law and order is important. As noted in Chapter 6, a variety of efforts are underway to reform and improve the methods of responding to wrongdoing.

Creating Safe Space

During war and violence, it is hard to gain perspective and make decisions objectively. People tend to go into survival mode and make reactionary decisions that may hurt their long-term interests. Fragile peace negotiations lose momentum with every suicide bombing on an Israeli bus and with every Palestinian house bulldozed to make way for Israeli settlements. Efforts to reduce violence create a space for cooling down and preparing for other approaches to peacebuilding.

The concept of safe space has three different dimensions. It is a physical place where people can meet across the lines of conflict. It's an emotional space where people have the time and focus to thoughtfully relfect on the choices they make about how to respond to conflict. And, it's a relational space that nurtures constructive interaction between people and conflict.

A variety of programs can help to achieve the immediate goal of reducing violence, thus making space for other peacebuilding approaches. These include legal and judicial systems intended to protect order and human rights, humanitarian relief aid, cease-fire agreements, peacekeeping, peace zones, and early warning programs to detect escalating conflict.

Systems and Approaches for Reducing Violence
Legal and Judicial Systems

Legal and judicial systems help to create order. When they are oriented toward justpeace, human security, and protecting human rights, they can help people to meet their own needs without interference from others. Legal and judicial systems should gain legitimacy through serving communities rather than through coercive violence. When they do not gain legitimacy in appropriate ways, however, they can contribute

> Laws and justice systems can help maintain order, which is essential for a sustainable peace.

to the problem. Legal and judicial systems are often the enforcers of structural violence that discriminate against and harm people based on their race, religion, class, or other identity. If legal and judicial systems are based on revenge, they can fuel and even increase the cycle of violence and crime within a society.

State-Based Law and Justice

The state system includes law enforcement, courts and some form of sanctioning or corrections. Ideally, these systems prevent individuals from hurting themselves and others, provide an opportunity for offenders to reflect on and change their behaviors, and encourage offenders to develop skills and ways of dealing with conflict so that they can make better choices. Such state-based legal systems are important for order and social control. However, in societies where these systems are ineffective or unjust, and where many citizens are not able to meet their basic needs, or where primary reliance is upon a "get-tough" approach, the task of maintaining order may become difficult. The only sure way to reduce crime is to increase the ability of people to meet their needs in ways that do not hurt others.

The concepts of community policing and restorative justice are growing in popularity and have a proven record of reducing crime. Community policing uses police partnerships that consult with and are accountable to the communities they serve. Restorative justice processes, described in more detail in the next chapter, are also increasingly used to address the problem of criminal and other offending behaviors in ways that promote community ownership and responsibility.

International Law and Justice

The founders of the United Nations responded to the horrors of World War II by establishing international laws and human rights to deter violent conflict and set standards for countries. These include international humanitarian laws establishing rules of war that seek to protect and limit harms to civilians during armed conflict.

In 2002, the United Nations established an international criminal court to hold people responsible for human rights crimes in countries that are unable or unwilling to do so. Earlier, two ad-hoc criminal courts were set up to judge war crimes in the former Yugoslavia and in Rwanda. While their effectiveness is controversial, these courts aim to affirm human rights, restrain offenders, and deter future people from participating in gross human-rights violations.

Humanitarian Assistance
Humanitarian aid seeks to relieve human suffering. It is important to peacebuilding because it can interrupt the cycle of violence that leads victims to commit revenge violence. Food, shelter, and medical aid offered by local religious and non-profit organizations assist victims of violence. In addition to providing important support for people in crisis, these organizations may also advocate for government and community responses to violence.

While international humanitarian aid is traditionally guided by principles of political neutrality and impartiality, recent research shows that this approach can exacerbate conflict if it turns a blind eye to politics. Aid is sometimes hijacked by warring sides, and profits are used to buy more weapons. Nevertheless, international humanitarian aid is important in meeting need and reducing violence. In fact, there is growing awareness that humanitarian aid processes, such as delivering food, organizing water and health programs in refugee camps, and building new housing provide an important opportunity to collaborate across the lines of conflict.

Cease-Fire Agreements

The first step in formal negotiations is to gain agreement between fighting groups to stop the violence. While cease-fire agreements do not address the roots of the conflict, they aim to create a safe space to allow further negotiations.

Groups engaged in warfare are willing to stop fighting when they experience a "hurting stalemate." This occurs when all groups are not able to gain more territory, when they are sufficiently tired of war, or when each group feels it has enough bargaining power at the negotiating table.

Without a cease-fire agreement, it is difficult if not impossible to negotiate about more difficult issues such as governance. If groups continue to fight during peace talks, people traumatized by new rounds of violence are unlikely to support the peace talks.

Military Intervention

Militaries everywhere claim to promote peace by reducing other people's violence. In the United States, arms manufacturers advertise warships as tools for diplomacy and nuclear weapons as "peacemakers." As an institution, the military is designed to be a last resort when diplomacy fails. The United States justified war on Iraq as necessary to protect human rights and security. But many peacebuilding actors debate the rules for and effectiveness of humanitarian military interventions. Using military force to reduce other people's violence inevitably harms civilians and often fails to protect human rights or security.

Still, others argue that militaries can contribute toward peacebuilding if they orient themselves toward peace enforcement missions and operations that respect local populations and humanitarian law. They point to examples such as the 2004 U.S. military presence in Haiti when internal conflict threatened to break into mass murder, and also to the 2003 U.S. military presence in Liberia that aimed to reduce levels of direct violence while relating respectfully to local populations. These uses of the military more closely resemble peacekeeping rather than traditional military strategies designed to defeat opponents.

Peacekeeping

Peacekeeping aims to stop the cycle of violence between armed groups using a variety of means. Peacekeepers may not only physically position themselves between armed groups, but they may also observe, document, and monitor violence. They may alert a network of supporters to exert diplomatic pressure on armed groups and their funders, facilitate communication between warring groups, monitor elections, and show solidarity with local people to demonstrate international support.[9] Each of these tasks is important to other peacebuilding activities. Military and civilian peacekeeping efforts share these goals and tasks but use different means to coerce groups to stop fighting.

At the international level, the United Nations and regional organizations use *military peacekeepers.* They often act as international police to maintain cease-fires, limit violence, and assist in withdrawing troops and demobilizing armed groups. Peacekeepers also may protect civilian workers and accompany relief aid workers and resources to ensure their safe transportation.

While military peacekeeping is important, it also receives wide criticism. In the former Yugoslavia, there were too few peacekeepers to prevent massacres. In places like Sierra Leone and Cambodia, peacekeepers routinely raped local women or forced them into prostitution in exchange for food. In Cyprus, peacekeepers separating the two sides may have removed the urgency for a political solution.

Civilian peacekeeping—also called unarmed peacekeeping, peace teams, or third-party nonviolent intervention—performs many of the same tasks as military peacekeeping. Civilian peacekeepers position themselves between opposing groups in an effort to reduce or stop the fighting, creating both a moral and physical barrier between the groups. When Muslims and Hindus began fighting in the streets after India gained independence from Britain, Gandhi's *Shanti Sena* or "peace army" walked into the violence, encouraged rioters to disperse, and created opportunities for constructive communication between groups.

Intercessionary peacekeeping uses individual peacekeepers to accompany endangered people or groups to prevent violence against them. Some international human rights organizations provide accompaniment for local human rights workers who might be threatened or killed for their work. In Sri Lanka, Peace Brigades International provides 24-hour accompaniment for civilians who are afraid they may be killed for their work as labor activists, human rights lawyers, or political candidates or officials.

During a South African election, peace monitors from around the world stood with local people, documented violations, facilitated communication between conflicting groups, and provided a calming presence in a potentially volatile situation.

Peace Zones

In the midst of war, civilian safety is difficult to secure. Peace zones aim to create safe spaces for civilians during war. Villages, cities, or regions negotiate with armed groups to become peace zones and make it illegal for anyone to carry a weapon within the boundaries. Of course, if civilians are strategic targets in the eyes of military or rebel groups, peace zones are unlikely to be effective. If successful, peace zones can help de-escalate violence by affirming that all groups can work together to reach even a small agreement about where not to fight.

Early Warning and Response Programs

Identifying the patterns that lead to violence helps communities create the political will to address conflicts before they become violent. Early warning programs systematically gather information on specific indicators such as an increase in ethnic or religious polarization, political exclusion, political prisoners, arms trade, media propaganda, or the movement of soldiers. Early response programs aim to bring international attention and resources to a conflict before it erupts into mass violence. It is much less expensive and far more effective to address conflicts before people are traumatized, maimed, or killed, and before a country's infrastructure is destroyed by war.

> An ounce of violence prevention is worth a pound of post-violence peacebuilding.

The programs detailed in this chapter are essential to interrupting escalating cycles of direct violence. However, there are concerns that these programs often are not adequately linked to other peacebuilding programs. In some places, they may even work against other peacebuilding approaches. In many countries, nonviolent activists experience severe repression from legal and judicial systems. Peacekeepers and relief-aid workers are accused of putting Band-Aid solutions on problems whose underlying causes of conflict need to be addressed. Alone, efforts to reduce violence in the short term do not stop violence from recurring.

Programs aimed at reducing direct violence must be based on the values of human security and justpeace. They also must be located within a much larger peacebuilding framework that can address root causes. The next chapter looks at how processes that aim to transform the very nature of relationships contribute to addressing those root causes.

9.
Transforming Relationships

Transformation is a key principle of all peacebuilding programs. Peacebuilding seeks to transform individuals, families, communities, businesses, structures, and governments away from destructive expressions of conflict and toward constructive growth and development. A core task of peacebuilding is to transform relationships so that those who harm and destroy move toward meeting human needs and ensuring rights.

The processes in this category of peacebuilding create opportunities for people to forgive and reconcile with each other. Yet perfectly reconciled relationships are a long-term vision. The idea of reconciliation recognizes that there is a spiritual dimension to both conflict and peacebuilding.[10] The religious concept of *shalom* embodies this sense of right relationships. Forgiveness and reconciliation signal deep changes in the ways people relate to each other, but they are not requirements for transforming relationships.

Peacebuilding aims to foster relationships that reflect the core values of peacebuilding. These core values include meeting human needs and protecting human rights in a way that recognizes interdependence, promotes partnership among peoples rather than domination, and limits all forms of violence.

Like a table with three legs, right relationships require three interrelated support processes: healing trauma, transforming conflict, and doing justice.

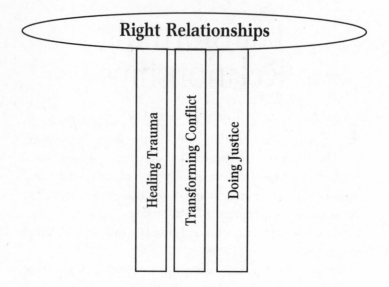

These processes use an array of relational approaches to address and achieve the three legs.

Trauma Healing

Trauma is an event, a series of events, or a threat of an event that causes lasting physical, emotional, or spiritual injury. Trauma can result, for example, from structural violence, crime, abuse, or acts of war. Some traumas stay with people for years or even centuries.

Chosen traumas are past traumas kept alive from generation to generation—sometimes over centuries—and are used as a rallying cry to spark new waves of revenge violence.[11]

People have different ways of responding to trauma, but some patterns emerge. Beginning with physiological effects, stress hormones flood the body and people feel shock and pain. Then people move to asking questions such as "Why me?" and often feel shame and humiliation about their victimization. As they begin to process the violence, they may become depressed, desire revenge, or both, feeling that revenge will alleviate their depression.

Trauma healing and recovery processes are an essential part of peacebuilding. The field of trauma healing seeks physical, emotional, and spiritual healing. It provides a space for people to identify harms and assert their needs. It can prepare individuals and communities to meet other people involved in or related to the offense, even the offenders themselves.

> Traumatic experiences leave people with lingering needs and wounds.

Trauma healing depends on building relationships and reconnecting people to their own sense of self, to the spiritual dimension, to other people, and to their environment. It helps the body discharge the physiological effects of trauma. Often this happens as victims form a community of survivors and find some relief in sharing with others who have experienced similar violence and loss. Trauma healing processes help people take constructive steps to prevent themselves and others from suffering further trauma.

Trauma healing uses a number of principles.

Principles of Trauma Healing and Recovery
- Name the trauma.
- Work through emotions and physiological effects.
- Find spiritual meaning.
- Form meaningful relationships with others.
- Re-establish a sense of personal control.
- Seek root causes of the trauma and work to alleviate them.[12]

Without trauma healing and recovery programs, or at least sensitivity to victims' needs, other peacebuilding processes such as humanitarian aid, peacekeeping, or even negotiation may be more difficult. Without healing, the experience of trauma can lead to offending behaviors; it is no accident that so many victimizers have themselves been—or perceive themselves to still be—victims. Trauma healing programs help victims identify themselves as survivors capable of being active peacebuilders to change their situation.

Conflict Transformation

Conflict transformation processes use democratic communication to address the underlying causes of conflict and create satisfactory solutions for all parties. Conflict transformation centers on several principles.

Principles of Conflict Transformation
- Identify experiences and issues that have caused a sense of harm, trauma, and injustice.
- Build relationships between people in conflict, which hopefully lead to forgiveness and to a process of reconciliation.
- Develop creative solutions that meet everyone's needs.

- Empower all people involved to transform their own conflicts.

Conflict transformation processes are needed at all levels to prevent and end violent conflict. These include efforts by international diplomats; politicians and policy-makers; business, religious, and media organizations; and community-level leaders.

Conflict transformation processes are not just useful among warring groups. They are also helpful among allies. Diversity and conflict thrive as much within the Israeli and Palestinian communities, for example, as between the two sides. Conflict transformation processes help build effective coalitions and democratic negotiating opportunities within as well as between various sides of a conflict. These skills and processes are also necessary within and between peacebuilding organizations to improve coordination and build constructive relationships. The following are some of the approaches used in conflict transformation.

Approaches in Conflict Transformation

Dialogue

The process of dialogue brings together groups of people to meet under the guidance of a facilitator to address important issues and increase understanding. Dialogue is an essential element in democracy. It is particularly important for communities that face an urgent problem, need to make an important decision, have experienced or are threatened by violence, or are experiencing increased hostility among members.

Formal dialogue processes invite people to share personal experiences, perceptions, and beliefs to gain a deeper understanding of the issues. They build cross-cutting relationships in divided societies. Preferably, such dialogue groups are sustained over a long period of time and help the group take action to address issues. Dialogue processes seek to increase communication and build relationships between people with different experiences and views. They help people gain a greater appreciation for the complexity of conflicts and lead to greater ownership and the capacity to address the structural dimensions of conflict.[13]

Principled Negotiation
Dialogue that is geared directly toward finding a solution to a conflict is negotiation. People negotiate informally all day long in their workplaces and as they conduct business and political deals. The field of conflict transformation seeks to move people away from "soft" forms of negotiation, where people may be too "nice" to assert their own needs and desires; and away from "hard" negotiation, where people neglect relationships in order to try to achieve their own goals at the expense of others. "Principled" negotiation is a set of strategies to build and maintain relationships with others while seeking creative win-win solutions that satisfy the needs of all.[14]

Mediation
Mediation is a process of guided negotiation assisted by a trusted person. A mediator helps people in conflict share their perspectives and experiences, identify underlying needs, brainstorm about creative options for addressing needs, and then make a final agreement. Like principled negotiation, mediation seeks to mutually satisfy needs in a win-win sustainable solution.

Training

In general, training programs belong in the capacity-building category of peacebuilding. However, training is also an intervention used to transform conflict. Under the guise of learning communication and negotiation skills, many training workshops for groups in conflict end up being a forum for building relationships, identifying key issues, and developing options for addressing the roots of violent conflict. Problem-solving workshops are a form of training where participants from different sides of a conflict learn skills to help them analyze key issues and solve problems creatively.

Doing Justice

While the previous chapter identified the role of legal and judicial systems in reducing violence, this chapter discusses their capacity to transform relationships. Where people can be identified clearly as victims and offenders, formal legal and criminal justice systems play an important role in establishing order and doing justice. However, these systems can also be unjust and rarely focus on healing or transforming people and relationships. They are also of limited value when victims and offenders cannot be clearly identified.

Restorative and transitional justice processes identify the harms, needs, and responsibilities of the people involved in conflict and/or crime, and create solutions that meet those needs.

Restorative Justice

Restorative justice processes can serve either as an alternative or as a supplement to state-based criminal justice systems. The latter tends to focus on identifying what laws have been broken, who broke them, and how the state should punish the offender. While this approach has some advantages, a key weakness is that offenders are held accountable to the state instead of to their victims. Victims are usually left out of the process of justice completely, and their needs and traumas are not addressed. Offenders are not encouraged to understand and address their responsibility to those they have harmed.

Restorative justice engages people in joint processes of identifying obligations and responsibilities resulting from injustice or violence, meeting needs, and promoting healing. Restorative justice focuses on the needs of victims, such as information about the crime, a place to tell their story of victimization, truth telling by the offenders, empowerment in the justice process, and restitution by offenders to victims. In some restorative justice processes, offender needs and the deeper causes of their behavior are also explored. In *The Little Book of Restorative Justice*, Howard Zehr suggests that restorative justice focuses on these questions:[15]

Key Questions of Restorative Justice
- Who has been hurt?
- What are their needs?
- Who is obligated to meet those needs?
- Who has been impacted or has a stake in this situation?
- What processes can be used to involve these stakeholders in finding a solution?

Transitional Justice
Transitional justice programs operate in post-war contexts where governmental authority is weak or

non-existent, particularly in societies emerging from war or dictatorship. Transitional justice programs include setting up new legal and judicial systems that integrate the needs and desires of local people, cultures, and institutions based upon international human rights laws and standards. They attempt to do justice with a view toward making peace. Increasingly, they include a truth and/or reconciliation commission that uses some restorative justice principles.

Truth and reconciliation processes aim to identify people or groups that attacked civilians, and to give victims a process to identify their needs and to receive symbolic and financial reparations. The sheer number of offenses and the delay in investigations into war crimes make identifying offenders difficult, time-consuming, and expensive. Offenders are often unwilling to confess their crimes for fear of punishment and because they see their actions through the lens of self-defense or as an effort to achieve their own sense of justice.

Truth and reconciliation programs such as the South African Truth and Reconciliation Commission (TRC) may offer human rights violators some sort of amnesty in exchange for their admission of guilt. Amnesty programs give individual offenders incentives to reveal the facts of their crimes needed by victims and their families. A compromise between amnesty programs and punishment-based justice may include more steps for holding offenders directly accountable to victims and for making reparations to them.

Governance and Policymaking

Relationships are at the heart of governance and policymaking. Government is a structure for guiding how people will relate to each other and make decisions through laws and regulations. Governments are responsible for making policies on issues that affect people. Active civil society groups support policymaking by gathering key stakeholders, analyzing important issues, and developing creative proposals for addressing public concerns. Environmental conflicts, for example, are increasingly dealt with through public processes that include all stakeholders and seek solutions that meet the interests of all groups.

Ritual and Symbolic Transformation

The processes described in this chapter rely heavily on verbal communication. Yet many people describe a sense of futility in trying to put their experiences of violence or their needs into words. Rituals and symbols are forms of communication that help people express themselves. In many formal peace talks, facilitators organize elaborate meals for participants. In trauma healing work, candlelight, prayers, or ceremonies help people feel safe to express their emotions and share their trauma. In the courtroom, symbols of justice help mark the special authority and seriousness of doing justice.

Ritual can be a helpful tool to assist and mark the process of transformation. Ritual helps transform people's identity from being victims of trauma to survivors of trauma. In mediations, a closing ritual can help people identify themselves as fellow problem-solvers rather than parties to a conflict. In some cultures, traditional rituals of sacrificing a bull or goat, drinking a special tea or liquor, or holding a formal ceremony are essential to peacebuilding. The formality of ritual can symbolize that a peace agreement is taken seriously and that people are entering into it with honest intentions.[16]

The processes covered in this chapter are essential to peacebuilding; in fact, they form the heart of it. The quality of the relationships between peacebuilders and the communities they serve impacts how effective they will be in mobilizing the communities where they work. Without the skills and processes to address trauma, transform conflicts, or restore a sense of justice, communities cannot create a culture of peace or support democratic governments that actively protect human rights. Yet, alone, these processes are still not enough. The next chapter moves toward an even bigger picture—the structures, institutions, policies, and organizations that shape the ways cultures respond to conflict.

10.
Building Capacity

Beyond ending violent conflict, peacebuilding also seeks to create the capacity for a *culture* of justpeace. Societies reflect a culture of peace and justice when they address the needs and rights of all people and are fully capable of expressing conflict through democratic processes. Rather than seeing culture as static, building the capacity for a justpeace requires people to know how to take responsibility for shaping their culture and all of their society's architecture, including structures, institutions, policies, and organizations that support it.

Capacity-building programs create communities and societies that are able to accept the challenge of long-term planning. The idea of long-term planning seems like common sense, but in reality public policy is usually driven by urgent crisis-response rather than thoughtful planning for the future. It usually takes as long to end a conflict as it took to create it. Often this is a matter of decades rather than months or years.

Sustainability is a key principle of this category of peacebuilding. It implies long-term thinking and planning, creating constructive relationship patterns between people and their environment, and developing the human resources and abilities to meet human needs for many generations. Capacity building includes training and education programs, development, transformation, and conversion of military structures to focus on human security and research and evaluation.

Approaches to Building Capacity

Education

Ideally, all forms of education provide individuals with the values and skills needed to live peacefully with others. Education includes informal socialization in the family, the media, and culture; formal schooling; and religious education. Each type of education has the potential to foster love and respect between people and can be a critical influence in building peace. Education can empower people to shape their environment and make a positive impact on the world around them.

Specific forms of education are particularly essential to building communities and societies with a capacity for peace. *Peace education* explores the causes of conflict and the conditions of peace. *Conflict transformation training* provides an opportunity to learn analytical, communication, and relationship skills. *Human rights education* seeks to empower people to know and articulate their human rights and helps people know how to use international laws and judicial systems to protect these rights. *Environmental education* increases awareness about the impact of human activity on the environment and about sustainable ways humans can live with minimal negative impact on the environment.

The media is a form of education as it provides information and shapes people's worldviews. Peace media programs aim to provide objective information about violent conflicts, help people recognize propaganda, and increase awareness about peaceful alternatives. In Rwanda and Burundi, peace programs on the radio provide an alternative to the call to violence and hatred put forth by other media outlets.

Development

Development is an ongoing process aimed at promoting human prosperity, happiness, and the quality of life. Development aims to strengthen communities' capacity to meet people's human needs and protect their rights. Development and peace are interdependent. War hinders or reverses development. Development, on the other hand, can help sustain and nurture peace.

The field of development is struggling to define its role in peacebuilding. Some prefer to focus on the goal of meeting human needs while avoiding peacebuilding processes that deal with political issues such as the arms trade, ethnic rivalry, or the lack of democracy. Others see the opportunity for development to contribute to peacebuilding by coordinating with other peacebuilding actors, fostering collaboration in divided societies, and addressing the structural roots of conflict.

Development facilitates innovation and the exchange of ideas about how to increase a community's capacity to fulfill human needs and protect rights. Development workers help communities identify solutions to their own problems, such as creating fair economic systems and reducing AIDS transmission, domestic violence, and other problems that cause suffering. Development organizations also facilitate the sharing and exchange of local innovations to other communities. By sharing such ideas and drawing upon local resources, development empowers communities to address their own problems.

Development comes in many forms. *Economic development* seeks to create businesses and financial institutions that help people meet their basic material needs. Economic development comes in different forms. One form, globalization, is criticized as being unjust because it enriches international corporations while increasing or doing little to alleviate poverty. The processes of globalization often lure poor people away from their villages to live in urban slums and work for as little as one or two dollars a day. Other forms of economic development, such as setting up micro-credit loans and fostering sustainable forms of agriculture and appropriate harvesting of environmental resources, seem to more concretely reduce poverty.

Political development seeks to ensure that community and national leaders have the skills to guide fair processes of decision-making and that institutions are in place to facilitate those processes. Governments gain legitimacy through the rule of law and broad citizen participation. Democratic institutions and processes guard people's freedom to engage in activities designed to bring about change through verbal communication rather than military means. Basic security is essential to the political arena, as it allows minority and opposition groups to safely voice their opinions. Political development uses national conferences or forums as well as community-level dialogue to address important issues.

Social or community development aims to improve the capacity of communities, civic and religious organizations, and other civil society actors to work together to address issues. Programs include leadership training, dialogue, organizational development, and the creation of civil society organizations and institutions.

Reconstruction is a form of economic, political, and social development geared for societies in a post-war context. In the post-war context or reconstruction phase, governments seek to replace and repair damaged infrastructure so their economies can recover.

Development programs can offer one of the most important opportunities to build relationships and trust between conflict groups. Groups in conflict may, in fact, be much more interested in working together to build a school for their youth or to learn the skills of micro-enterprise than they may be to sit down at a dialogue aimed at reconciliation. Sometimes conflicts get transformed when the focus is not on the conflict itself but on a shared goal, such as improving the quality of life.

The field of development, like other forms of peacebuilding, can also have a negative impact. Development aid can increase violence if it is used to benefit some groups and not others. Large amounts of development aid are stolen by corrupt officials in receiving countries and even may be used to buy arms to fuel conflicts. Some governments give aid for development projects that benefit producers in their own countries yet actually harm receiving countries by flooding their markets with foreign products that put local farmers out of business.

Military Conversion

Some peacebuilders focus on changing the nature of military institutions in their efforts to build a culture of justpeace. Military conversion programs aim to increase civilian authority over the military, refocus military trainings and tasks on human security, channel military resources and budgets toward human security goals, and support international disarmament. They support the development and use of nonlethal weapons to immobilize and capture offenders without harming civilians.

In the United States, military conversion efforts focus on changing the existing military structures so that they embrace a larger human security agenda that focuses on global human needs and rights in addition to national security interests. Groups such as the U.S.-based Center for Defense Alternatives examine current security threats, particularly since September 11, 2001, and provide detailed suggestions for changing U.S. military policy and infrastructure to better address global rather than national security concerns. They also proposed strategic alternatives to the U.S.-led war on Iraq. Another organization, the Coalition to Oppose the Arms Trade (COAT) works to transform military industries and bases to civilian uses and seeks to provide alternative employment for those serving in the military or employed by arms manufacturers.

In the post-war context, military conversion programs demobilize, resettle, and retrain former combatants to live and participate in their communities. Peacebuilders work at demobilization in countries such as Liberia and Sierra Leone, where large militaries oppressed local populations.

Research and Evaluation

Research contributes to peacebuilding in several ways. Researching the dynamics and causes of conflict can alleviate the conflict as people involved in the process gain greater insight. Evaluative research aims to learn from current and past efforts to build peace. What worked? How did it work? What did not work?

Research is also used to develop new tools, methods, or projects for peacebuilding. Development agencies research better ways to get clean water to remote communities, prevent the spread of HIV/AIDS, or deliver food aid so that it becomes a community-led, cooperative effort that contributes to peace. Think-tanks, or research institutions, develop proposals for democratic governance to use in different cultures and create economic models for how to focus economies on meeting human needs while providing capitalist incentives for innovation and hard work. Other research institutions create designs for developing transportation, homes, and industries that can use renewable energy sources.

The capacity-building programs described in this chapter plant the seeds for a culture that supports just-peace. This fourth category of peacebuilding has the potential to put the other three categories of peacebuilding out of business. If every community and nation educated its citizens for peace and contributing to the common good; focused on economic, political, and social development; converted its military focus to human security; and engaged in ongoing research to improve the quality of life, there would be less structural and direct violence and less need for short-term solutions to these problems. Combining the four categories of peacebuilding covered in these last four chapters requires strategic design tools, the subject of the next chapter.

11.
Strategic Design of Peacebuilding

Just days after the September 11, 2001 tragedy, my husband, daughter, and I traveled to Fiji to help facilitate a national peace conference. Overwhelmed with the events in my own country, I struggled to formulate a hopeful, welcoming speech to the participants. In the end, I read a quote from a Latin-American peacebuilder about planting date trees. Roughly summarized, the quote urges people to plant the seeds now for the trees that will bear fruit in generations to come.

Planting the seeds of peace requires strategy. The key tasks of peacebuilding include: making decisions about what we need to do to make that dream possible; imagining who can plant the seeds and nurture this dream; and proposing when, where, and how the planting should happen. My colleague and mentor John Paul Lederach uses a set of strategic frameworks to make decisions about the what, who, when, where, and how of peacebuilding.[17] His work forms the organizing framework for this chapter. Under each subtitle that follows, a variety

---

of tools are offered for helping peacebuilders make strategic decisions. Each of these tools has strengths and weaknesses, so they are best used in conjunction with other tools.

The Strategic "What"

How do peacebuilders decide what to do? A variety of analytical tools are useful for strategically designing a coordinated series of peacebuilding programs based on available resources, needs, and key issues that have the capacity to draw people's energy and attention. Each of these tools is briefly reviewed here.

A Local Capacity for Peacebuilding

A focus on local capacities or resources for peace is an important first step. Only local people can create the road maps to their future. It is important to identify local people, programs, systems, symbols, attitudes, and traditions that help connect people and sustain an architecture of relationships to support peace.[18] The focus on local capacities for peacebuilding aims to build on and enhance what is already working and minimize possible harm and failure of peacebuilding activities initiated from the outside. It sees local culture as a resource for peacebuilding. It seeks to learn from the past and takes seriously the challenge of making all peacebuilding actors responsive to local cultures.

A second approach for identifying what can build peace is known as *appreciative inquiry* or *assets-based assessment*. This method appreciates and assesses what is already happening by asking key questions that can help people think about their situation in a new way. Rather than focusing on problems, positive approaches to peacebuilding seek to discover the successes and strengths that can be built upon and supported through peacebuilding interventions.[19] Similarly, the Listening Project methodology uses non-threatening interview and dialogue processes to allow people to express views and solutions to issues in their community.

Needs Assessments

Needs assessments help communities discuss their needs while laying out a variety of options for meeting those needs. Needs assessments can help communities identify where they need to build their own capacity and how they can meet their own needs. The violence map on page 24 can help communities name the various types of violence they are experiencing. The peacebuilding map on page 26 can serve as a needs assessment tool for communities to assess what interventions or peacebuilding programs are already happening in their communities and what could be developed as part of a peacebuilding strategy.

Connectors and Dividers

Each community has a set of systems, institutions, attitudes, values, experiences, symbols, and occasions that connects and divides people. Connectors, like common music or language, act as bridges between people in conflict. Dividers, like war propaganda or ethnic prejudice, contribute to conflict. Peacebuilding strategies must support and increase connectors and inhibit or stop dividers. [20]

Framing

Peacebuilding requires strategic choices about how to frame issues in ways that will mobilize people to act.

Frames are like different lenses. They provide language, metaphors, and theories for people to understand a large complex issue. Gandhi was an expert framer, tackling the goal of decolonization through a series of smaller issues, such as the right for Indians to make their own salt or wear their own traditional clothes. For many people, talking about peace and reconciliation signals compromise and selling out to the other side. Talking about peacebuilding in terms of a strategy for long-term security or terror prevention is sometimes an easier sell. Finding the best frame or doorway to talk about an issue makes a tremendous impact on how people respond. Sometimes framing is done best in an impartial way, appealing to all parts of the political spectrum.

The idea of framing issues is related to John Paul Lederach's concept of a "presenting situation," a particular crisis or aspect of a conflict that catches our attention.[21] Presenting situations, like a specific rape in a community, make people aware of a problem. It is a starting point to talk about problems that may have much deeper roots and histories, such as media portrayal of women and sexist attitudes.

Persuasion and Coercion

Peacebuilding processes use both coercive and persuasive methods to bring about change. Deciding whether to use persuasion, coercion, or both in a peacebuilding strategy requires careful analysis of the situation.

Persuasion invites people to change by convincing them that it is in their interest to do so. This happens through self-reflection, building relationships, and exchanging experiences and ideas. When people voluntarily choose to change their minds and behaviors as a result of learning through negotiation or dialogue, they are more likely to feel good about the change, and the change in their behavior is more likely to be lasting.

Yet persuasion alone does not always work. Martin Luther King Jr. said it like this: "Freedom is never voluntarily given by the oppressor; it must be demanded by the oppressed." Coercion forces people to change by making them "hurt" through social, psychological, political, economic or physical isolation, pressure, or force. While violence itself is coercive, there are also nonviolent means of forcing change. Coercive peacebuilding strategies include human rights actors who mobilize shame by economic sanctions or boycotts, and civilian peacekeepers who try to force groups to stop fighting.

Yet coercion alone does not solve problems or bring a sustainable peace, and some coercive strategies may be counterproductive. The application of coercive and persuasive strategies requires keen judgment and precise timing. This topic is revisited in the "Strategic When" section.

Levels of Transformation

Lederach argues that peacebuilding requires fostering transformation at personal, relational, cultural, and structural levels.[22]

- **Personal change** includes new attitudes, behaviors, and knowledge by individuals within the context.
- **Relational change** includes new or improved relationships between groups within the context.
- **Cultural change** includes strengthened values that support peace.
- **Structural change** includes new institutions, policies, and/or leaders.

Levels of Transformation

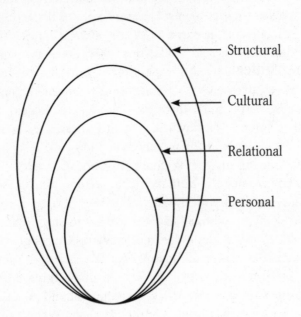

Each peacebuilding program or activity may not address all of these levels. However, a coordinated peacebuilding strategy will address all levels through various programs. For example, in Rwanda some groups focus their work on individual trauma healing and on tolerance programs aimed at helping people reflect on their own attitudes. Other groups carry out dialogue programs to build relationships between groups at the community level. International peacebuilding organizations such as Search for Common Ground are focusing on cultural change by creating radio soap operas that emphasize peaceful values and skills. Finally, the United Nations and the Organization of African Unity are working at structural change to create a new set of leaders who are able to work together across the lines of ethnicity and conflict. Some research shows that programs aimed at individual change contribute to sustainable peacebuilding only when they are explicitly linked to structural change goals.[23]

The Strategic "Who"

Peacebuilding is everyone's responsibility. Deciding who to draw into peacebuilding processes requires more strategic decision-making.

Multi-Track Diplomacy

Governments are responsible to provide safety and security to their citizens. But governments are not solely responsible or capable of building peace. During the Cold War, a number of nongovernmental efforts to build relationships between the Soviet Union and Western states gave credibility to the peacebuilding roles of individual citizens and broader civil society actors. These nongovernmental efforts came to be known as Track II and they complemented Track I or state diplomacy.

The concept of multi-track diplomacy acknowledges the diversity of actors in Track II, including the media, conflict resolution professionals, businesses, religious organizations and leaders, activists, private citizens, researchers, educators, women, youth, and traditional leadership structures.[24]

Traditional leadership, such as elders, chiefs, and kings, exists in many communities around the world and has a wealth of traditional ceremonies, rituals, and precedents for building peace in their communities. In many South Pacific islands, for example, it would be impossible to consider excluding elders, chiefs, and local kings from peacebuilding processes between the various ethnic groups. Local people respect these local authorities as much as, if not more than, that of state governments. In Western societies, local religious or community leaders may play a similar role. Recognizing the various actors in peacebuilding calls for coordination and collaboration between tracks.

Key People and Critical Masses

The strategic "who" of peacebuilding requires determining which actors can instigate significant change. Lederach uses two metaphors to describe how key people can mobilize large numbers of people for peace.[25]

Key people are like yeast in a bread recipe. The quantity of yeast in comparison to flour is small, yet yeast makes the rest of the bread grow. It has the capacity to bring about great change.

Key people may also be like a siphon. Siphons work by moving small amounts of a liquid through a tube using suction. Once a small amount of liquid is pulled, the rest of the liquid follows, moving from one container to another.

Determining the strategic "who" requires an analysis of which people or groups can act as the initial liquid through the tube or the yeast in making bread. These leaders are sometimes called the opinion makers, because they shape the opinions of their followers.

Key leaders are important for peacebuilding in two ways. First, they may have the authority and opportunity to make important decisions that can reduce violence and address basic needs. Second, they may be able to use their influence to create a critical mass where so many people embrace their ideas and solutions so that change is inevitable. The media, education, and other processes can also help create a critical mass of people committed to peacebuilding.

Vertical and Horizontal Capacity

Peacebuilding actors operate at different levels of society. Lederach uses a pyramid to illustrate.[26] At each level of the pyramid, there are people capable of inspiring and leading social change efforts. At the top level, the United Nations, national governments, and religious leadership such as the World Council of Churches participate in official dialogue, negotiation, and mediation to address conflicts such as a political crisis. At the middle level of the pyramid, national and regional organizations and businesses lead policy and program initiatives, such as providing the regional coordination for relief aid for a humanitarian crisis. At the grassroots or community level, a variety of local groups carry out relief and development programs, civilian peacekeeping, dialogues, trauma healing, training and education programs, and other projects.

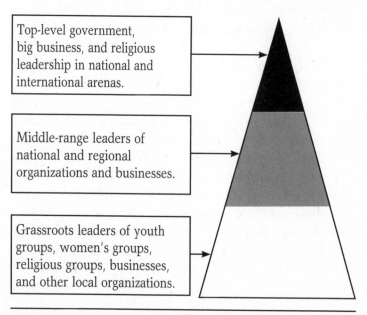

Top-level government, big business, and religious leadership in national and international arenas.

Middle-range leaders of national and regional organizations and businesses.

Grassroots leaders of youth groups, women's groups, religious groups, businesses, and other local organizations.

For example, in the 2004 humanitarian crisis in Sudan, many actors at various levels were involved. Peacebuilding efforts at the top level included personal appeals by U.N. Secretary General Kofi Annan for the Sudanese government to address and acknowledge the widespread famine. At the middle level, groups such as Oxfam and the Red Cross mobilized international and regional resources and coordinated efforts for relief aid. At the local level, grassroots nongovernmental organizations and churches worked together to deliver the relief aid and to set up feeding camps.

Lederach proposes four key principles for working with these three levels:[27]

1. A **horizontal capacity** for peacebuilding is a set of relationships within each level of the pyramid that allows leaders to coordinate with each other in peacebuilding programs across lines of conflict, ethnicity, religion, or other social division. Most current peacebuilding programs foster horizontal capacity. People-to-people dialogues between citizens from India, Pakistan, and Kashmir, for example, develop a vision and capacity for working together for change when they come together to share their experiences of violence. As a result of these grassroots dialogues, local communities are learning how to respond to crises in order to prevent violence. For example, a group of Muslim and Christian women in Nairobi, Kenya's largest slum meet regularly to share information about potential violent conflicts in their community and plan for how to intervene immediately to quell tensions.

2. A **vertical capacity** for peacebuilding is a set of relationships between top, middle, and grassroots leaders that recognizes their different and interdependent contributions to peacebuilding. Increasingly, people at all levels are recognizing the need to have relationships with people working at other levels. For example, the United Nations is increasingly showing interest in working with regional organizations and their grassroots partners in setting up early warning networks to alert the international community to impending violence.

3. Those in the **middle level,** such as some business or religious leaders, are more likely to have access and relationships with those at both the top and grassroots levels. Working with the middle level, then, requires strategic planning to foster vertical cooperation. The West African Network for Peacebuilding is an example of a mid-level organization that has access both to grassroots people and groups working for change, and to high-level government and U.N. diplomats.

4. **Vertical and horizontal integration** is a set of relationships between individuals, networks, and organizations that allow people at all levels to work together for peace. Strategic peacebuilding fosters this type of integration at all levels of the pyramid as it seeks to bring about a just peace in a divided society. In the United States, vertical and horizontal integration of peacebuilding leadership would require grassroots groups working at racial reconciliation, for example, to connect with other grassroots groups *and* government, religious, and business

organizations at the middle and top levels to design a systemic approach to this historic conflict.

Moderates and Extremists

Peacebuilding requires including both moderates and extremists. Both leaders who instigate violence and those who already support peace need to be involved in peacebuilding processes. Far too many programs involve only those who are predisposed to peace. Pro-violence leaders are often left out as they are seen as "spoilers" capable of hijacking, sidetracking, or even rejecting peace processes. Yet if they are not included, peacebuilding programs have little chance of success.

Insiders and Outsiders

In most violent conflicts around the world, both insiders and outsiders are working for peace. They participate in peacebuilding in different ways. Insiders are people who live within the conflicted community and call it home. Insiders generally make a longer-term commitment to the work and have more at stake if peacebuilding succeeds or fails. They have a deeper understanding of local culture, context, the conflicts, and local resources for peace. They are more likely to hold credibility and trust with local people and to have extensive networks of relationships.

Outsiders are people and organizations who travel to the conflict region specifically to participate in peacebuilding. Outsiders are likely to have a larger set of economic and political resources. These resources allow them to raise international awareness about the conflict and about how local participants are working at peacebuilding. Outsiders can help influence national and international powers to address the conflicts and find funders to give financial resources. In addition, outsiders can increase the safety and political leeway for insiders to do their work by physically accompanying them to prevent retaliatory violence. They can also create space and support for conflict transformation, restorative justice, and trauma healing programs.[28]

The Strategic "When"

Conflict is dynamic; it changes over time and moves in waves and cycles. Peacebuilding seeks to prevent and address violent conflict. Peacebuilding needs to occur before, during, and after violence. The diagram below shows how strategic peacebuilding requires a variety of actions in each of these three time frames.

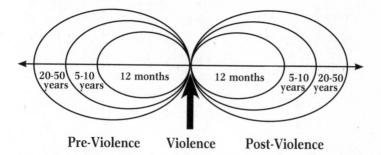

Pre-Violence   Violence   Post-Violence

Pre-Violence

Before violence breaks out, structural forms of violence often exist. One or more groups may perceive an unfair distribution of resources or a violation of human rights. Preventative peacebuilding programs intervene before mass violence erupts. Early warning and response projects aim to monitor conflicts in their early stage and send an alarm to the international community, governments, and nongovernmental organizations before violence begins. Through advocacy and other forms of strategic action, nonviolent activists can wage conflict by drawing national and international attention to important issues and to the need for structural change. International, national, and community leaders can work together to express and address the issues democratically, convincing people that negotiation rather than violence is the best means for resolving the conflict.

Violence

During times of direct violence, additional peacebuilding programs need to address victims and offenders. International and local aid agencies need to create shelters for displaced people and other victims of the violence. Offending groups must be stopped by peacekeepers or police and restrained from committing further violence. Leaders at all levels need to urgently create opportunities for people to build relationships across and within the lines of conflict and to address the underlying needs of all groups in conflict. They must work toward finding mutually satisfactory solutions to immediate problems. If violence continues for many months or years, long-term capacity-building programs are needed to train people in human rights, conflict transformation, restorative justice, and other areas.

> Conflicts are "ripe" for negotiation when power is roughly balanced and there is wide awareness of the key issues.

Post-Violence

After war, societies need to disarm and reintegrate armed people, address traumas, and rebuild infrastructure. Capacity-building programs can help societies develop ongoing peace and human rights education, create opportunities for social and economic development, and channel research funds into creating democratic structures that are culturally based.

Evaluating Conflict Ripeness

Knowing when the time is right for intervention requires an analysis of how aware people are of the issues and how much power each group has relative to others. Negotiation is not always possible. Sometimes groups in power refuse to negotiate with others.

For example, before the Civil Rights Movement in the United States, the African-American community was significantly disempowered in relation to the white state and national governments. The Civil Rights Movement used demonstrations, vigils, pilgrimages, and sit-ins to create mass awareness of the injustices facing African Americans and to demonstrate the power of the black community. Over a period of many years, the Civil Rights Movement "ripened" the conflict to a place where white leaders had to pay attention and negotiate with African Americans to address their concerns. As a result of many negotiations and court cases, segregation laws were changed, civil rights laws were enacted, and many white Americans began to understand and challenge the attitudes and structures of racism.

The diagram on page 78 portrays how to determine whether a conflict is ripe for interventions.[29] In the lower left corner of the graph, power is unbalanced and awareness is low. Activist strategies use a mix of coercion and persuasion to wage conflict nonviolently. If these strategies work, power becomes more balanced, people's

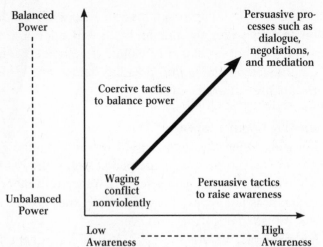

awareness of issues increases, and the roots of conflict and violence are addressed as relationships form through dialogue, negotiation, and mediation.

Symbolic Dates

Some dates have symbolic meaning. The launch of a new peacebuilding program, the signing of peace accords, or the arrival of peacekeepers can harness the symbolism of dates. Human rights groups use the symbolism of March 21, 1960, the date of the horrific Sharpesville Massacre in South Africa, to advance their International Day for the Elimination of Racism.

The Strategic "Where"

Strategic peacebuilding also requires an analysis of symbolic and socially-important places and spaces that can support relationship-building. If a peacebuilding program is to focus on youth, then schools, soccer fields, and playgrounds will be important places for intervention. Women will need to mobilize in places where they meet other women. In many developing cultures, women run the marketplace and have staged significant protests by mobilizing other women in this space.

Norwegian mediators took Israelis and Palestinian negotiators to rural chalets where they shared meals family-style and took hikes through the woods together. Creating a symbolic setting that encourages negotiators to find their common humanity is an important element in diplomacy at all levels.

The Strategic "How"

How will strategic peacebuilding take place? What are the core principles? What is needed to coordinate peacebuilding actors and activities? The following principles suggest the primary steps or tasks in designing a peacebuilding strategy.

Principles of Strategic Peacebuilding Practice

1. **Reflect on values.** Peacebuilding requires ongoing personal and organizational reflection, clarification of guiding values, and an evaluation of how peacebuilding programs fulfill those values.

2. **Analyze conflict and violence.** Peacebuilding requires ongoing analysis of the resources needed for peace, and of the causes and dynamics of conflict and violence.

3. **Address basic needs and rights.** Peacebuilding helps people to meet their own basic needs and rights while acknowledging the needs and rights of others.

4. **Plan long term.** Peacebuilding moves beyond a short-term, crisis orientation toward designing social change over years and decades.

5. **Transform whole systems.** Peacebuilding includes changes at the personal, relational, cultural, and structural levels.

6. **Coordinate approaches and actors.** Peacebuilding requires coordinated approaches that reflect responsibility, ownership, accountability, and participation by many different actors.

7. **Identify and create power.** Power exists in all relationships. Peacebuilding requires all people to be aware of their power and to use that power nonviolently to meet their human needs while respecting others.

8. **Empower others.** Peacebuilding strengthens and builds upon local efforts and empowers others to act. Peacebuilding is based on participatory democracy and self-determination.

9. **See culture as a resource.** Cultural values, traditions, and rituals can be resources for peacebuilding.

10. **Innovate and use creativity.** Peacebuilding uses multiple ways to communicate and learn rather than relying only on words or dialogue to develop creative solutions to complex problems.

12.
Evaluating and Coordinating Peacebuilding

At least one measure of the success of peacebuilding is the sheer number of people who devote their lives and careers to building peace. In 1980, no university offered degrees in conflict transformation and peacebuilding. Today, many universities offer at least a class on the topic of the relational skills of peacebuilding, and dozens offer bachelors, masters, and doctoral degrees. At the community level, hundreds, if not thousands, of peacebuilding workshops and trainings take place all over the world. The large numbers of trained people influence the language and awareness of others. Today virtually every United Nations program is linked to the concept of peacebuilding, and government leaders in many countries are requesting training.

Yet the spread of an idea is only one indicator that an approach is actually successful in meeting its goals. Peacebuilding programs do not always contribute to peace. Good intentions are not enough. Some peace-building programs waste time and financial resources and increase prejudice or even violence. Peacebuilders have a responsibility to evaluate their programs to ensure that they are not doing harm and are using their resources wisely.

South Africa is a model of success for many peace-builders. Thousands of South Africans attended peace-building trainings and participated in a variety of programs to address community-level and national conflict. The end of apartheid is a significant shift toward just-peace, as it increased political equity. However, it did little to change economic inequities between black and white South Africans. An inability to address economic structures that continue to benefit whites disproportionately feeds a sense of despair, humiliation, and increased criminal, domestic, and sexual violence among poor communities.

One key challenge is to create evaluation tools that adequately measure movement toward peace. If violence and peace are opposite ends of a continuum, early warning indicators such as increased political exclusion and unemployment signal a move toward violence. Indicators of peace—the opposite of early warning indicators—include increased political networking and employment opportunities. These indicators can help peacebuilders reflect on the effectiveness of their programs.

The second challenge for peacebuilders is coordination. The success of peacebuilding is ultimately linked to the ability of individuals, groups, communities, and nations to work together in planning and pursuing a justpeace. Coordination and planning pull the strategic what, who, when, where, and how together into a comprehensive peacebuilding plan. Without coordination, different approaches to building peace may contradict other approaches or simply fail to achieve their maximum impact.

Yet coordination poses significant challenges to peacebuilders. Coordination cannot simply be one organization or group directing or delegating tasks to others. Ideological differences, ego-driven efforts to monopolize peacebuilding programs, and competition for resources are potholes on the road to peace. Peacebuilding actors need to work together to create coordination networks that model, practice, and hold each other accountable to jointly-defined peacebuilding values, relational skills, analytical tools, and processes.

Such coordination will require ongoing conversations about guiding values and analytical frameworks for understanding conflict and violence. It requires forums to collaborate and share innovations, practices, failures, and success stories. It will also require positive relational skills at all levels, particularly among the people and organizations that may compete

> Without coordination, different approaches to building peace may contradict other approaches or simply fail to achieve their maximum impact.

and conflict with each other in the process of building peace. Lastly, it will require coordinating the practice of peacebuilding so that groups working at short-term, immediate programs take into consideration the needs and goals of longer-term peacebuilding programs. Funders can facilitate coordination by requiring attendance at inter-agency forums and by building an environment where organizations are rewarded for cooperating with each other rather than competing for funding and fame.

This book has laid out a framework for peacebuilding that requires coordination of many different actors and approaches to many important issues over decades rather than months. We cannot do it alone—peacebuilding requires a generous spirit among the peacebuilders: holding tongues that unfairly criticize the work of others, and communication skills and processes that enable peacebuilders to address the conflicts among themselves. All of our seemingly disparate efforts can be part of a unified effort, provided we work together toward a common goal of justpeace.

Endnotes

1 Lisa Schirch, "A Peacebuilding Framework to Link Human Rights and Conflict Resolution" in *Human Rights in Conflict* (Washington, D.C.: U.S. Institute of Peace, Forthcoming 2005).

2 Vern Neufeld Redekop, *From Violence to Blessing* (Ottawa: Novalis, 2002).

3 James Gilligan, *Preventing Violence* (New York: Thames and Hudson, 2001), 39.

4 Robert J. Burrows, *The Strategy of Nonviolent Defense* (New York: Statue University of New York Press, 1996), 239.

5 Gene Sharp, *The Methods of Nonviolent Action* (Boston: Porter Sargent Publishers, 1973).

6 Robert F. Drinan, *The Mobilization of Shame: A World View of Human Rights* (New Haven: Yale University Press, 2001), 32.

7 Gene Sharp, *The Politics of Nonviolent Action* (Boston: Porter Sargent Publishers, 1973).

8 Peter Ackerman and Jack Duvall, *A Force More Powerful: A Century of Nonviolent Conflict* (New York: Palgrave, 2000).

9 Lisa Schirch, *Keeping the Peace: Exploring Civilian Alternatives to Violence Prevention* (Uppsala, Sweden: Life and Peace Institute, 1995).

10 Hizkias Assefa, "Peace and Reconciliation as a Paradigm" in *Peacemaking and Democratization in Africa,* Hizkias Assefa and George Wachira, eds., (Nairobi, Kenya: 1996).

11 Vamik Volkan, *Blood Lines: From Ethnic Pride to Ethnic Terrorism* (Boulder: Westview Press, 1997).

12 Seminars on Trauma Awareness and Recovery (STAR) manual. Eastern Mennonite University, 2002.

13 Harold Saunders, *A Public Peace Process: Sustained Dialogue to Transform Racial and Ethnic Conflicts* (New York: Palgrave, 1999).

14 Roger Fisher and William Ury, *Getting to Yes: Negotiating Agreement Without Giving In* (New York: Penguin Books, 1991).

15 Howard Zehr, *The Little Book of Restorative Justice* (Intercourse, Penn.: Good Books, 2002).

16 See Lisa Schirch, *Ritual and Symbol in Peacebuilding* (Bloomfield, Conn.: Kumarian Press, Forthcoming 2005).

17 This chapter relies heavily on John Paul Lederach, *Building Peace: Sustainable Reconciliation in Divided Societies* (U.S. Institute of Peace, 1997), and unpublished handouts on strategic peacebuilding.

18 Mary B. Anderson and Lara Olson, *Confronting War: Critical Lessons for Peace Practitioners* (Cambridge, Mass.: Collaborative for Development Actions, Inc., 2003).

19 *Positive Approaches to Peacebuilding: A Resource for Innovators,* ed. Cynthia Sampson et al. (Washington, D.C.: Pact Publications, 2003).

20 Mary B. Anderson, *Do No Harm: How Aid Can Support Peace—or War* (Boulder: Lynne Rienner, 1999).

21 John Paul Lederach, *The Little Book of Conflict Transformation* (Intercourse, Penn.: Good Books, 2003), 34.

22 John Paul Lederach adapted from Maire Dugan in "From Issues to Systems" in *Mediation and Facilitation Manual* (Mennonite Conciliation Resources, 2000).

23 Anderson and Olson, 2003.

24 Louise Diamond and John McDonald, *Multi-Track Diplomacy: A System's Approach to Peace* (Bloomfield, Conn.: Kumarian Press, 1996).

25 John Paul Lederach, "Strategic Concepts and Capacities for Justpeace" (Handout for Fundamentals of Peacebuilding class, Eastern Mennonite University, 1999).

26 John Paul Lederach, *Building Peace: Sustainable Reconciliation in Divided Societies* (U.S. Institute of Peace, 1997), 39.

27 John Paul Lederach, "Strategic Concepts and Capacities for Justpeace" (Handout for Fundamentals of Peacebuilding class, Eastern Mennonite University, 1999).

28 Anderson and Olson, 2003.

29 Adapted from Adam Curle, *Making Peace* (London: Tavistock Press, 1971).

Selected Readings

Anderson, Mary B. and Lara Olson, *Confronting War: Critical Lessons for Peace Practitioners* (Cambridge, Mass.: Collaborative for Development Action, Inc., 2003).

Galama, Anneke and Paul van Tongeren, eds., *Towards Better Peacebuilding Practice* (Utrecht, Netherlands: European Centre for Conflict Prevention, 2002).

Lederach, John Paul, *Building Peace: Sustainable Reconciliation in Divided Societies* (Washington, D.C.: U.S. Institute of Peace, 1997).

Lederach, John Paul and Janice Moomaw Jenner, *Into the Eye of the Storm: A Handbook of International Peacebuilding* (San Francisco: John Wiley and Sons, 2002).

Reychler, Luc and Thania Paffenholz, eds., *Peacebuilding: A Field Guide* (Boulder: Lynne Rienner, 2001).

Sampson, Cynthia, Mohammed Abu-Nimer, Claudia Liefbler, and Diana Whitney, eds., *Positive Approaches to Peacebuilding* (Washington, D.C.: PACT Publications, 2003).

About the Author

Lisa Schirch is an associate professor of peacebuilding at Eastern Mennonite University's Center for Justice and Peacebuilding. A former Fulbright fellow, Schirch has 15 years of experience consulting with a network of strategic partner organizations involved in peacebuilding activities throughout the United States, Latin America, Africa, Asia, the South Pacific, and Europe. Her peace-building experiences include working in a refugee camp, organizing a human rights campaign, acting as a civilian peacekeeper, living in remote villages as a development field worker, consulting as an evaluator and researcher of development and peacebuilding projects, facilitating inter-ethnic dialogues, and ongoing work as a mediator and trainer. She holds a Ph.D. in conflict analysis and resolution from George Mason University.

Group Discounts for

The Little Book of
Strategic Peacebuilding
ORDER FORM

If you would like to order multiple copies of **The Little Book of Strategic Peacebuilding** by Lisa Schirch for groups you know or are a part of, use this form. (Discounts apply only for more than one copy.)
Photocopy this page as often as you like.

The following discounts apply:

1 copy	$5.99
2-5 copies	$5.39 each (a 10% discount)
6-10 copies	$5.09 each (a 15% discount)
11-20 copies	$4.79 each (a 20% discount)
21-99 copies	$4.19 each (a 30% discount)
100 or more	$3.59 each (a 40% discount)

Prices subject to change.
FREE shipping on orders of 100 copies or more to continental U.S.

Quantity   *Price*   *Total*

____ copies of **Strategic Peacebuilding** @ _____ _____

(Standard ground shipping costs will be added for orders of less than 100 copies.)

TOTAL _____

METHOD OF PAYMENT

❒ Check or Money Order
   *(payable to **Skyhorse Publishing** in U.S. funds)*

❒ Please charge my:
   ❒ MasterCard   ❒ Visa
   ❒ Discover   ❒ American Express

\# _____

Exp. date and sec. code _____

Signature _____

Name _____

Address _____

City_____

State _____

Zip_____

Phone_____

Email _____

SHIP TO: (if different)
Name _____

Address _____

City_____

State _____

Zip_____

Call: (212) 643-6816
Fax: (212) 643-6819
Email: bookorders@skyhorsepublishing.com
(do not email credit card info)